Crabs on a Rock

words by Josephine Croser
illustrated by Veronica Jefferis

Six crabs sat on a rock.

A dog took one.

Five crabs sat on a rock.

A bird took one.

Four crabs sat on a rock.

A wave took one.

Three crabs sat on a rock.

A fish took one.

Two crabs sat on a rock.

A net took one.

One crab sat on the rock.

It went off the rock.

It went under the rock.

It went into the sand.

Six crabs sat on a rock.